EASY FRENCH VOCABULARY GAMES

R. de Roussy de Sales

PASSPORT BOOKS
a division of *NTC Publishing Group*
Lincolnwood, Illinois USA

1991 Printing

Published by Passport Books, a division of NTC Publishing Group.
© 1988, 1983, 1975 by NTC Publishing Group, 4255 West Touhy Avenue,
Lincolnwood (Chicago), Illinois 60646-1975 U.S.A.

0 VP 9 8 7 6 5 4 3

PREFACE

Experience has shown that entertaining games and puzzles are an effective means for helping beginning French-language learners build their vocabulary. No one need tell you that vocabulary is basic to your mastery of French. So, a book that allows you to acquire a solid base of French vocabulary *without* dry memorization is a valuable learning tool indeed!

The 48 anagrams, acrostics, word mazes, and cryptograms in *Easy French Vocabulary Games* are designed to give you some very useful practice with about 600 important French words. As you go through this book, you will find that this varied array of word games will tease you into remembering or deducing the meanings of French words. Most puzzles are based on a specific topic that is essential to learning and speaking French. Subjects such as numbers, days of the week, months of the year, family members, colors, and so on are important areas for the beginner to master. Here, they can be learned with a maximum of fun and effectiveness. Games are accompanied by complete instructions and, in most cases, have been started for you, so that there should be no doubt about how to play.

To help you check answers, a complete list of the French words used in this book and an Answer Key have been provided at the back of the book. After you have completed these games, you will find detailed instructions for creating your own word puzzles. So, the fun can continue long after you have solved the puzzles in this book.

Now, go to it! We're confident that *Easy French Vocabulary Games* will not only amuse you, but help you acquire lasting knowledge of the French language.

SENTENCE MAZE

How good are you at following a trail? Suppose the trail is
a French sentence wandering around the maze on this page?
Could you start with the letter P at the top of the maze and
move from letter to letter -- in any direction except diagonally -- spelling out the words in the sentence until you
come to the last letter of the last word, which is the framed
S in the center square? Remember, the letters spelling out
the words may run from left to right, from right to left, up
or down. You'll have to watch out for false starts which will
fizzle out on you, and you may not skip over any letters in
your path.

When you have finished, you will have a complete French
sentence, beginning with P, ending with S, and pointing out
one reason for exercising your French vocabulary with
puzzles like these.

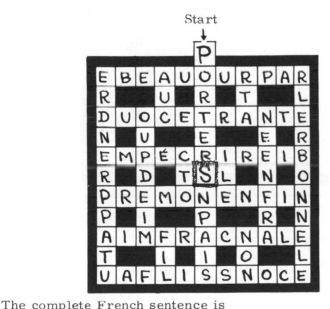

The complete French sentence is

"_____

_____

_____"

SCRAMBLED GRAMMAR

A typesetter in an old-fashioned printing shop was setting up type for a page of grammatical terms in a French text-book. Turning suddenly, he accidentally knocked the type he had already set to the floor. Some of the pieces were lost in the shuffle, but others stuck together in twos and threes. After picking up all he could find, the typesetter found that by using some of the groups of letters more than once, he could still put together <u>ten</u> French words having to do with grammar.

How many of the ten can you put together in two minutes?

sub   stan   sent   in   plu   lier   tif   fini   ti   el   voy   con   elle   ter   ad   jug   ver   jec   gu   min   sin   aison   be   pré

1. _____ 4. _____ 7. _____

2. _____ 5. _____ 8. _____

3. _____ 6. _____ 9. _____

10. _____

FRENCH ANAGRAMS

Suppose you were playing anagrams in French, and had the
letters below to make French words out of. How many of the
French words suggested by these English "daffy-nitions"
could you find? The number of squares after each hint will
tell you how many letters in the French word you are to
guess.

C I R S F A E R S N U E T O M L

1. He knows all about you and likes you anyway!.. `A m i`

2. This makes its mark in the classroom...

3. Oh, how you hate to get up in this!.......

4. What you usually get for nothing...........

5. This runs up and down in front of your house...

6. They say this makes the world go 'round!

7. A hot drink and a place to get it............

8. Your French book is full of these.....

9. This is what most of us live in........

10. Thirty days have most of these.............

11. The blue over all.........................

12. The last thing that women always want.........

P.S.: No. 12 is a dirty trick, but think
how smart you'll feel when you
get it!

3

DIFFERENCE OF OPINION

You have already made the acquaintance of cognates, words which are spelled the same way in English and French and which have similar or identical meanings. You may also have noticed that, in some cases, while French words are spelled exactly like certain English words, the meanings are distinctly different. Just for the fun of it, how many of the following pairs can you identify?

1. What French word meaning a window-shade is an English word for a hoard or supply? _____

2. What French word meaning a public way is an English verb meaning to regret? .. _____

3. What French word meaning the end is an English word meaning a fight? . . . . _____

4. What French word meaning a thing is a form of an English verb meaning selected? _____

5. What French word for an intersection is an English word for a piece of money?... _____

6. What French word meaning a large ripple is an English adjective for indefinite?... _____

7. What French word for "the staff of life" is an English word meaning suffering?.. _____

8. What French word meaning well-behaved is an English word for wise man?........ _____

9. What French word for a precious metal is an English conjugation meaning else?... _____

10. What French word for a kind of fruit is an English adjective meaning a shade of red? _____

ODD WORDS

In each of the following groups of French words, there is
one word which does not fit in the group. For example, in
a group of words including "blanc, noir, joli, rouge, vert,"
the word "joli" is out of place because all the other words
are names of colors. In the same way, one word in each of
the groups below will stand out because it is not related to
the others. When you have decided which is the odd word,
write the first letter of that word on the blank at the right of
the line. When you have finished, you'll find that you can
rearrange the letters in the blanks so that they will spell
out still another French word. Can you figure out that word
and write it on the line at the bottom of the page in the time
allotted?

Write first
letter of
"odd" words
here ⟶

1. assiette.. serviette.. cuillère.. tasse.. rideau.. verre._____

2. lampe.. chaise.. une.. table.. piano.. sofa......... _____

3. cahier... papier.. nous.. encre.. plume.. crayon..... _____

4. va... avec... met... dit... est... voit............. _____

5. viande... salade... café... tarte... livre.. potage..._____

6. jouer.. infinitif.. substantif.. pluriel.. verbe.. pronom_____

7. leçon.. grammaire.. classe.. élève.. ouvert.. maîtresse

_____

The French word which can be
spelled by rearranging the first
letters of the odd words is _____

5

ACROSTIC PROVERB

Here is another sort of acrostic for you to try your French hand at. You have eighteen numbered blanks, which, when filled in the letters they represent, will spell out a French proverb. To help you get the letters, you have sentences containing key words made up of the same letters which spell out the words in the proverb. Your problem is first to guess the words in the key sentences (the number of blanks will show you how many letters in each!), fill them into the blanks, and then transfer the letters one by one into the correspondingly numbered blanks in the proverb itself.

When you have finished, you will find that the French are a persistent sort of people who believe that you should keep right on trying, because--

V _ _ _ _ l _   C' _ _ _   _ O _ _ _ l _.
1 2 3 4 5 6 7   8 9 10 11   12 13 14 15 16 17 18

Key Words:

V O l C l un problème pour vous!
1 13 6 8 17

Un _ _ _ est une petite pièce de monnaie française.
   10 16 3

Le _ _ _ _ _ _ est un musée fameux à Paris.
   4 2 14 15 7 9

On ne peut pas avoir _ _ _ _ d'amis.
                      11 18 5 12

6

FRENCH RUNDOWN

In this puzzle, what you are going to try to do is to guess a number of French words belonging to a certain category or classification, and then fill them into a puzzle block vertically, in such a way that one letter from each of the words you guessed will furnish one letter in a key word describing the group as a whole. A sample puzzle has been worked out for you around the kind of things that might be found in the livingroom. As you can see, when the words "chair," "rug," "lamp," "sofa," and "piano" are fitted together vertically in the right order, the key word SALON can be spelled out in one horizontal row. Study the sample for a moment to see exactly how it works:

Then try your hand at the same sort of arrangement, built around a number of French COLORS! How many of them can you think of which can be put together
    like
      this----

A word to the wise:

Some colors will fit in two different places. Others won't!

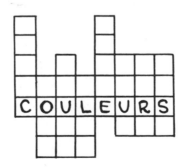

ETTE-IQUETTE

The ending "-ette" seems to be a popular one for French words, since you have already learned a number of them which end in these letters. How many of these "-ettes" can you ferret out from the hints given below?

1. What "-ette" is used to hold food?....... _____

2. What "-ette" is worn on the head?...... _____

3. What "-ette" is a piece of meat? .... _____

4. What "-ette" is a bar of candy?........ _____

5. What "-ette" has four tines?........... _____

6. What "-ette" has two wheels?.......... _____

7. What "-ette" is folded at the table?..... _____

8. What "-ette" flies over water?......... _____

9. What "-ette" is demonstrative?........ _____

10. What "-ettes" are worn on the nose?... _____

****

P. S. What "-ette" is a well-known French folksong?

QUICK CHANGE

To perform the sleight-of-hand tricks below, you will have to start by guessing one French word, and then by changing only one letter in that word, turn it into another French word as suggested by the English clues. The first quick change has been pulled for you. How long will it take you to pull off the rest?

In other words BY CHANGING ONE LETTER can you...

1. Turn a fruit into a man?..... P O M M E → H O M M E

2. Turn one parent into another? .

3. Make a prize of peace?........

4. Make a city of a thousand?..

5. Make a basket of paper?..

6. Turn a hat into a castle?

7. Bring fires from your eyes? ..

8. Change x to (x + 4)? ....

9. Make the best of the old?....

10. Make mine yours? ....

11. Make a map of a dessert?...

12. Turn your hand to bread?....

P. S. Here's a tricky one. Can you think of a way to make property vanish?...

9

SHADES OF MEANING

Comprenez-vous les homonymes homographes? You never heard of them? Shame on you! Everybody -- well, practically everybody, that is -- knows that homographic homonyms are words which are spelled exactly alike but have different meanings. At any rate, whether or not you could live for the rest of your life without worrying about homographs, here's a quick quiz on some French ones for you to try your hand on. In each of the following French sentences, the blanks can be filled in with two words, spelled and pronounced alike, but meaning two different things. See if you can guess what they are from the meanings of the sentences. The number of blanks in each word will show you how many letters in the words to be puzzled out.

1. S O U S la table, j'ai trouve six S O U S.

2. Nous n'avons pas___ en classe pendant l'_____.

3. Elle est_____ intelligente que sa sœur, et elle est très jolie, _____.

4. La salade servie par la_____est très_____.

5. Pas tout le_____peut voyager dans tous les pays du_____.

6. __ janvier, nous voyons beaucoup de neige, mais en juillet, il n'y__ a pas.

7. Cet homme est très pauvre. Il y a_____ans qu'il n'a pas acheté pas un habit____.

8. Les élèves ne doivent_____oublier qu'un_____ d'interrogation s'emploie à la fin d'une question.

9. Les hommes sont quelquefois plus_____que les_____ de la forêt.

10. Dans les régions du____, il fait très chaud à____.

FRENCH TRELLIS

A French Trellis is one part crossword puzzle and one part vocabulary quiz. The problem is to find exactly the right place to fill in French words answering the definitions given, so that when you have finished, all the words will be filled into the puzzle in an interlocking pattern. Each French word will, of course, fit exactly in only one place, and when correctly placed, will give you leads to new ones. The French word for "book" has been filled in to give you a start. It should give you clues toward locating a 4-letter word beginning with L, a 7-letter word with V as the 4th letter, and a 4-letter word ending with E. Things should move pretty fast after that!

3-letter words
Myself
Belonging to us
Indefinite article
Who

4-letter words
Nothing
Distant, far
Under
Expensive, dear
That
To tell or say

5-letter words
Morning
Also
Road, way
Book
They
Earth, land

6-letter words
Ancient, old
A number

7-letter word
New

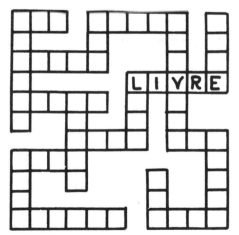

WORD MAZE

This word maze contains the french names for eight different animals, four of which are common domestic animals, and the other four the kind you wouldn't particularly care to meet unexpectedly! You can spell out the French words for these animals by moving in a continuous path from letter to letter in the maze below. You may start in any square, move in any direction, horizontally, vertically or diagonally; but you may not skip over any square to get to another, and you may not enter any one square more than once in the same word.

To give you a push in the right direction, suppose you look carefully at the upper right hand section of the maze and see if you can't make out one of the four wild animals running around the corner!

Quatre animaux domestiques:

1. _____

2. _____

3. _____

4. _____

Quatre animaux sauvages:

1. _____

2. _____

3. _____

4. _____

ARTISTIC FRENCH NUMBERS

Here is a study in concentration -- and confusion! But it will give you a chance to show how well you can read French numbers! In the mass of numbered dots below, you are to start with number <u>one</u> and draw a continuous line from number to number <u>in the order given in the column at the left</u>!

When you have finished (if you have managed to hang on around the curves) you will have outlined a somewhat impressionistic rear view of a cuddly animal.

Allons! En chasse!

un
douze
trente
quatre
quinze
seize
soixante-dix
huit
dix-neuf
dix
onze
deux
treize
quarante
cinq
six
dix-sept
quatre-vingts
neuf
vingt
soixante et onze
vingt-deux
trois
quatorze
cinquante
soixante
sept
dix-huit
quatre-vingt-dix
vingt-quatre
soixante-quinze
quarante-deux
trente-trois

quarante-quatre
cinquante-cinq
soixante-six
soixante-seize
quatre-vingt-dix-neuf

WORD-GO-ROUND

At least 35 French **words overlap each other** in this spelling-
go-round. How many of them can you find? Just start at any
point on the circle and move clockwise around it, writing
down all the French words you can spell out without skipping
any letters. You may count all kinds of French words, nouns,
adjectives, prepositions, articles, contractions, even
different forms and tenses of verbs. In other words, if it is
a French word, it counts, just so long as it has two or more
letters in it, and you do not skip around or move backwards.
The blanks for your words are arranged so that you may turn
the book as you go around the circle and still write conveniently.

How about starting off with <u>ma</u>, <u>mai</u>, <u>ai</u>, ----------?

You may add any
accents you need!

SCRAMBLED NATIONS

Whatever they may look like, the groups of letters below are perfectly good French words. It's just that they've been jumbled up some. Rearrange the letters in each group and you can spell out the names of ten different countries of the world. How many can you unscramble?

MAGLENALE _____ _____

RETNAGELER _____ _____

USISES _____ _____

CARFEN _____ _____

LAITIE _____ _____

SURISE _____ _____

GAPSENE _____ _____

PONAJ _____ _____

SETTA-NISU _____ _____

ADANCA _____ _____

INTERLOCKING CIRCLES

Here are some English hints or suggestions which will help
you to guess twelve four-letter French words. Each word
encircles its own numbered square, either in clockwise or
counterclockwise direction, and at the same time inter-
locks with the words beside, above and below it. The first
two words have been filled in to start you off. How long will
it take you to find and fill in the rest?

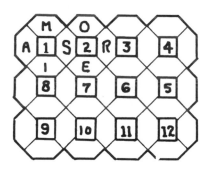

Remember!

Either ↻ or ↺ !

1. A big conjunction

2. Both a color and a
   flower

3. Half-way between
   black and white

4. You and I

5. The color of most newspaper print

6. Large and heavy

7. All by yourself

8. Between today and
   tomorrow

9. How you're doing in
   French, no doubt!

10. One thing you'll learn to
    do in French

11. The main thing you use
    your eyes for

12. How you did this puzzle,
    we trust!

ACROSTIC PROVERB

The twenty-five numbered blanks below can be filled in with
letters which will spell out an old French proverb. Where do
you find the right letters? You get them from the key words
answering the definitions below the blank (temporarily, of
course) proverb!

As soon as you have thought of a French word answering the
definition given and with as many letters as the number of
blanks indicates, you will fill it in, first in the key word,
and then in the correspondingly numbered blanks in the proverb itself. The first key word has been solved and filled
into the blanks for you to show you the way. Now see how
long it will take you to work out a proverb which would seem
to indicate that the French don't care about Rome, the
important thing is that----

_ _R_ _ _ _ _ _ _ _ _T_
1 2 3 4 5   6 7 8 9 10 11 12 13

F_ _ _ _ _ _ _ _ _O_ _
14 15 16 17 18 19 20 21 22 23 24 25

FORT : strong; very
14 23 3 12

_ _ _ _ _ : a period of time
7 19 21 11 18

_ _ _ _ : a month of the year
22 24 16 6

_ _ _ _ _ : left; departed (participle)
8 2 25 17 4

_ _ moins : at least
9 20

_ _ _ _ _ : past; out of date
1 15 5 10 13

17

WORDS IN WORDS

This is a simple sort of word game, in which you are to try
to guess two French words suggested by an English tipoff.
The trick is that one of the words is inside the other! You
do not have to rearrange the letters or unscramble them.
If you have correctly guessed the longer word, you will see
the shorter word spelled out by letters within it. Or maybe
you can guess the shorter word, and then build the longer one
around it. The puzzle squares will show you the number of
letters in the longer word, as well as the location of the
inner one. Try it?

1. Inside this color, you'll
   see a masculine article......... `B L E U`

2. Here's another color with a
   feminine article..........

3. This is a piece of French money
   that covers a period of time.....

4. Inside another period of time
   there is a part of the body........

5. This is a public square with a
   body of water in the middle......

6. This one is a day of the week
   which has a number in it........

7. There is probably someone in
   the world, don't you think?......

8. This is forever and a day,
   with the day in the inside........

9. Strange that such a small number
   should surround a monarch......

10. And how about finishing with a
    question containing a direction?.

18

SQUARE CHAIN

These nine English clues should suggest nine French words
which can be arranged in the diagram in such a way that
each word will run completely around one block of squares
and provide the first letter (in the numbered square) for the
next word in the chain. The first word will run only around
the first block of squares. Thereafter, each word will start
with the letter in the numbered square, run across the bridge,
and clockwise around the next block of squares.

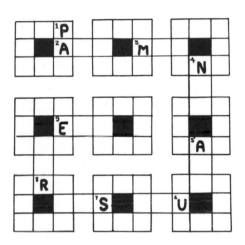

1. The easiest answer
   to "Why?"

2. Positively! No
   doubt about it!

3. At this very
   moment

4. What breathing is
   to all of us

5. The best day for
   something wonderful

6. An institution of
   higher learning

7. What "surprise parties"
   are supposed to do

8. What you don't like to
   do to trouble

9. Precisely

LOST VOWELS

The strange conglomerations of letters below can be read as perfectly good French sentences, except for the fact that in each of the sentences some one vowel has been omitted all the way through! All you have to do is to decide what vowel has been lost, insert it in all the proper places, divide the letters into words, accent and punctuate, and VOILA! To help you get going, the first sentence has been started for you. The missing vowel in this one appears to be e. With e's inserted in all the right places, the sentence begins to take shape with "Les bons élèves--". Can you go on from there?

L S B O N S L V S T U D I N T L U R S
L C O N S P O U R T R B I N P R P A R S

LES BONS ÉLÈVES ÉTUDIENT

_____

_____

L G R M M I R E N E S T P S F C I L E M I S
I L F U T L S V O I R P O U R P R L E R
B I E N L L N G U E F R N C I S E

_____

_____

L E S T D F F C L D E L R E A N S S V O U S
N A V E Z P A S D M A G N A T O N

_____

_____

S I V O S A P P R E N E Z Q E L Q E S
N O V E A X M O T S T O S L E S J O R S
V O S A R E Z B I E N T O T N V O C A B
L A I R E P L S T I L E

_____

_____

_____

20

DIFFERENCE OF OPINION

This is a quick quiz on words which are common to both English and French, but which have different meanings in the two languages. The English questions are designed to give you leads to the words to be guessed. In each case, the question can be answered with one word, which is both English and French, but which will mean one thing to a Frenchman, and something else again to an American or Englishman. How many of the ten do you know?

1. What French word for a color is
   an English word for a cosmetic?.......... _____

2. What French word for a number is
   an English word for a small coin?........ _____

3. What French word for a tower is
   an English word for a trip?............. _____

4. What French word for an animal is an
   English word for informal conversation?.. _____

5. What French word meaning to eat is an
   English word for a place where animals go? _____

6. What French conjunction is an English word
   for a means of transportation? .... _____

7. What French word for a writing tool is
   an English word for a feather?.......... _____

8. What French word for a speech is an
   English word for a conditional pardon?.... _____

9. What French word for a part of the body
   is an English word referring to all of it?.. _____

10. What French word for an ordinal number
    is an English word for a statesman?...... _____

21

CRYPTO-FRENCH

The coded words below are the French names for seven
different fruits. They are written in what is called a simple
substitution code. That is, other letters of the alphabet have
been used all through the list to stand for the real letters of
the words.

Look down the list, thinking over the names of fruits you
know in French and see if you can spot one which you can
recognize by the arrangement of letters in it. Suppose, for
instance, that the first one is a very common fruit in which
the third and fourth letters of its French name are the same.
Think you could guess what that could be? Go ahead! Take
a chance! Fill in the correct letters in the blanks below the
coded ones. Now you know what C stands for in this code.
Run down through the other coded words and everywhere you
find a C, fill in the letter you've decided it is substituted for.
Do the same with B, N and V. When you have decoded these
letters wherever you find them, you should have a good
start on one or two of the other fruits.

Allons-y!

FRENCH RUNDOWN

If you had been working the sample puzzle below, you would have been told to think of the French words for some of the things which might be found in the livingroom, and fit them vertically into the puzzle blocks in such a way that one letter from each word could be used to spell out the word SALON. The words for "chair," "rug," "lamp," "sofa," and "piano" solved the puzzle very nicely, as you can see. Study the sample puzzle for a moment and you will see just how it was done.

How about trying the same sort of stunt with the French names for the MONTHS OF THE YEAR? If you will juggle them around a little, you'll find they can be fitted into this pattern:

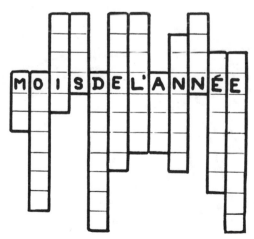

WORD-GO-ROUND

How many overlapping French words can you find in the wheel of letters below? There are at least 44 there, if you can spot them. Just start at any point in the circle, and without skipping any letters, move clockwise around the circle, spelling out as many French words as you can recognize. You may use any word of two letters or more. Suppose, for example, that you started at the arrow at the top of the circle. You should be able to spot "table" and "tableau" right away, and if you look carefully, you can see "blé," "le," and "eau." Get the idea? The blanks for your words have been arranged so that you can turn the book and still write conveniently. Carry on!

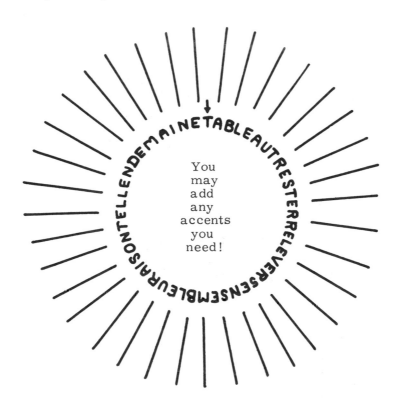

You may add any accents you need!

24

SENTENCE MAZE

In the labyrinth of letters below, there is one--and <u>only</u> one---
complete French sentence. It starts with the letter <u>L</u> at the
top of the maze, runs from letter to adjoining letter, and ends
with the letter <u>U</u> in the large center square. Sometimes the
letters spelling out the words of the sentence run from left to
right, sometimes from right to left, sometimes up, and
sometimes down. In other words, you may move in any direction, so long as you do not skip over any square to get to
another, and so long as the letters keep spelling out French
words. Watch out for wrong turns which will try to lead you
off into dead ends! When you have finished, you will have a
complete French sentence, which begins with the letter L,
ends with the letter <u>U</u>, and expresses a <u>very</u> profound thought!

Hang on!   START

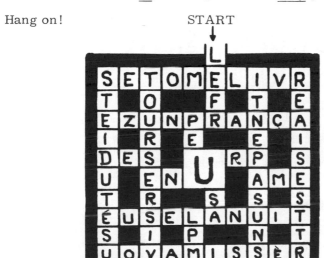

The complete French sentence is

"
_____

_____

_____."

ACROSTIC PROVERB

If you will begin by guessing the key words below, and
filling in the letters in the blanks, first in the key words, and
then in the correspondingly numbered blanks in the twenty-two
blanks marked "Proverb," you can spell out an old French
saying which appears to prove that the French do not believe
that "Absence makes the heart grow fonder."

The first key word has been filled in for you to start you on
your way.

Take it from there!

Proverb:

_O_ _ _ _ _ _ _ _ _ _X_ ,
1 2 3 4 5 6 7 8 9 10 11

_ _ _I_ _ _ _ _ _C_ _ _ _R_.
12 13 14 15 16 17 18 19 20 21 22

Key Words:

"_C_ _R_ _O_ _I_ _X_ de Guerre": a French military decoration.
18 22 2 14 11

_ _ : an adverbial pronoun
8

_ _ _ _ _ : a spot or place
12 3 9 21

_ _ _ _ : alone, by oneself
7 20 17 1

_ _ _ _ _ : awards, present (verb in the 3rd person
1 13 15 4 6   singular)

_ _ _ : twosome, duet (borrowed from the Latin!)
5 10 19

26

FRENCH TRELLIS

Below are the English meanings for 15 French words which can be fitted into an interlocking position in the puzzle pattern provided. Each French word will fit perfectly in only one place. The English definitions have been grouped according to the number of letters in the French words they represent. The French word RENTRER, answering the definition "to return," has been filled in to give you a starting place. Now you can see that the very bottom word in the puzzle is a 6-letter word with R as the 2nd letter. Look through the definitions for 6-letter words till you find the one that answers that description. If you can find it, you are ready to start hunting for a 4-letter word ending in R. Got it? All words run horizontally or vertically, just as in an ordinary crossword puzzle.

Definitions

4-letter words
So much
Blow, stroke
2nd person
Day

6-letter words
Money
To remain
Own, proper

5-letter words
Our
To hold
Wealthy
Full
A number
Small

7-letter words
To return (Key word)
To arrive

QUICK CHANGE

The "quick changes" in this puzzle are accomplished by guessing a French word which can be changed to another word <u>by the addition of one letter.</u> The letter to be added may be inserted anywhere in the word, but the position of the rest of the letters must remain the same. The English clues will give you leads to both words. Study the first pair of "quick-change" words and you will see how it is done. Then see if you can do it yourself. . .

BY ADDING ONE LETTER

1. Change a masculine article to a small body of land. . . . . `L E → Î L E`

2. Change a demonstrative adjective to a large round number. . . . .

3. Change them to those. . . . .

4. Change a foot-step to a country. . . . .

5. Change a part of the body to a part of the day. . . . .

6. Change a feminine article to a night light. . . . .

7. Change something you wear on your legs to another part of the body. . . .

8. Change give back to take. .

9. Change a masculine pronoun to a male descendant. . . . .

10. Change a short conjunction to a small piece of money. . . . . .

AN EAR FOR FRENCH

Here is a guessing game based on French words which are spelled differently and have different meanings, but are pronounced alike. The English questions contain definitions or hints which should help you to guess the French words. For example, in the first question, the French word for short story, conte, has the same pronunciation as the French word comte, which is the title given to a French count or earl. Can you go on from there?

1. What short story CONTE sounds like a nobleman COMTE?

2. What boy's name ▯▯▯▯ sounds like people ▯▯▯▯?

3. What member of your family ▯▯▯▯ sounds like a body of water ▯▯▯?

4. What possessive adjective ▯▯▯ sounds like a big hill ▯▯▯▯?

5. What summer month ▯▯▯▯ sounds like a conjunctive adverb ▯▯?

6. What color ▯▯▯▯ sounds like something to drink from ▯▯▯▯?

7. What inner craving ▯▯▯▯ sounds like the end ▯▯▯?

8. What part of the body ▯▯▯ sounds like a blow ▯▯▯▯?

9. What conjunction ▯▯▯ sounds like a fraction ▯▯▯▯?

10. What preposition ▯▯▯▯ sounds like a number ▯▯▯▯?

ODD WORDS

Here are seven groups of French words. In each group, all
of the words except one have some relationship to each other.
Your problem is to find the misfit or odd word. If, for example, you were looking for the word out of place in a group
of words including "blanc, noir, joli, rouge, bleu," you should
be able to spot the fact that "joli" is the odd word in the group,
since all the other words are French colors.

The words in the groups below are not quite as obvious as
all that, perhaps, but the same principle applies. Look through
each group of words and decide which of the words does not
seem to belong with the others. Draw a circle around the odd
word in each group. When you have finished, if you have been
right all the way, you will find that all of the odd words themselves have something in common. See if you can figure out
what it is.

1. médecin...avocat...artiste...fiancé...professeur

2. robe....manteau....début....bas....soulier

3. musique...encore...poésie...peinture...sculpture

4. ciel....terre....soleil....lune....suave

5. cinéma...première...hôtel...église...gare

6. matinée....vallée...montagne....fleuve....mer

7. café....biftek....mouton....porc....veau

Now! What do the odd words have in common?

LA SALLE DE CLASSE

Here's a cryptogram for you to decipher. Below are a number of French words for people and things to be found in a classroom. If they don't <u>look</u> like French words (or any other kind, for that matter!) it's because one straight line has been left out of every letter except the letter <u>I</u>. All you have to do is to decide which line is missing in each letter, draw it in with your pencil, and <u>voilà</u>! Remember, it's not always the same part of the letter that is missing. For instance, the letter <u>A</u> might be H, F, or ⊓ ; and F could be an A, D, or P, depending on where you draw the line!

The teacher has been put together as an example! The dotted lines are the ones which had to be added to make the word show up. How many of the others can you bring to light?

le P ROFESSEUR

l'ÉIÈ\Ξ

laLⴔⴔⴔⵏⵉΞ

le ⊓3_ΞⵏL

le 3ⵏPΞⵏⵏ

laLⵏⵏⵏ⊆⊆

la ⌐⊏P⌐Ξ

le _ⵏ\ PF

la ⸗ΞⵏⵏÊ⌐PΞ

le ⸗ ⵏⴔⵏ Uⵏ

le LPHΞ⸗

FRENCH RUNDOWN

Here's a kind of crossword puzzle that doesn't cross. The words run only one way -- vertically! Still, if you can guess the right words to fill in, and put them in the right places, one letter from each word will help to spell out a title fitting the group as a whole. In the sample puzzle given, for example, the words to be guessed were things that might be found in the living room. When the French words for "chair," "rug," "lamp," "sofa," and "piano" are filled into the right places, the word SALON is spelled out with one letter from each word. Do you follow?

Now try to think of the French words for as many family members and relatives as you can, and try to fit nine of them into this pattern!

Watch out for words that seem to fit in one place, but will make room for another if moved over!

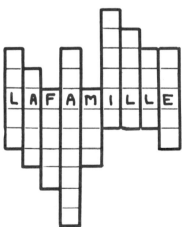

LETTER DESIGN

Here are eleven French words, each of which has seven
letters in it, and each of which contains the letters "-re-"
somewhere in its spelling. All you have to do is to fill in the
blanks! Of course, it would help some to have some hint as
to what the words mean! So you have, in the column on the
left, a list of definitions for the words -- in French! On the
other hand, in the column on the right, you have some extra
help in the way of the remaining letters in each word. The
only trouble is that they are not in the right order, so that
you will have to decide just where to fill them in. The first
word has been worked out for you. Look it over, and then
try the rest on your own!

French definitions for puzzle words:	Puzzle words:	Letters to be filled in:
Rendre plein..........	RE_ _ _ _ _	PLIRM
A peu près...........	_ RÈ_ _ _ _	QUESP
Faire rester en place..	_ _ RÊ_ _ _	TEARR
Content, joyeux........	_ _ _ RE_ _	UHEXU
Tirer de nouveau.......	_ _ _ _ RE_	TERIR
Ouverture dans un mur..	_ _ _ _ _ RE	TEFEN
Faire voir............	_ _ _ _ RE_	ROMNT
Effroi, répulsion.......	_ _ _ RE_ _	ROHUR
Le père et la mère.....	_ _ RE_ _ _	PANTS
Partie de la tête........	_ RE_ _ _ _	LILEO
Retourner	RE_ _ _ _ _	VERIN

SCRAMBLED PROVERBS

It's amazing how you can change the looks of a word by just
mixing up the letters in it! The French proverbs on this
page are all there, but the letters in each of the words have
been scrambled. The results are a little confusing at first,
maybe, but if you will be patient and use a little imagination,
you can rearrange the letters in each word and put them
back where they belong. Each word is scrambled separately,
and the spaces between words have been left as is, so that
when you have unscrambled each of them, they will read off
in their correct order in the sentence. The English hints
about the meanings of each proverb should give you some
help in straightening them out.

1. A famous English author used the English version of this
    French saying as the title for one of his plays:

    OTUT SET NEBI IQU NIFTI EBIN.

    Tout est ____ ____ ____ .

2. Maybe you should look before you leap, still, on the
    other hand, you must admit that--

    UQI EN QUIRSE NIRE A'N ERIN.

    ____ ____ ____ ____ ____ ____ .

3. The French, too, seem to find that troubles often seem
    to come in bunches:

    NU HUMERAL EN TENIV SAMAJI LUSE.

    ____ ____ ____ ____ ____ ____ .

4. What's that old English "saw" about a new broom?
    The French put it this way:

    UTOT VOENUAU, OTTU UBAE.

    ____ ____ , ____ ____ .

5. Maybe both languages should say "Live and <u>help</u> live"!
    At any rate, the French version goes --

    LI TAFU QUE UTTO EL DOMEN EVVL.

    ____ ____ ____ ____ ____ ____ .

34

WORD MAZE

How many parts of the body can you name in French?

By moving from letter to letter in the maze below, you can
spell out twelve such French words. Start with any letter in
any square in the maze and move from letter to adjoining
letter until you have spelled out the word you are looking for.
You may move in any direction, horizontally, vertically, or
diagonally; but you may not skip over any square to get to
another one, and you may not use any square more than once
in the same word.

Can you find French names for parts of the body?

R	S	T	U	E	Z
B	O	G	N	B	D
U	D	I	A	M	C
C	E	P	L	J	O
H	L	V	R	E	U

1. _____   5. _____   9. _____

2. _____   6. _____   10. _____

3. _____   7. _____   11. _____

4. _____   8. _____   12. _____

FRENCH TRELLIS

The French Trellis is nothing more than a vocabulary quiz
with a slightly different twist. All you have to do is to fit
the French words answering the definitions given into their
proper places. The words run either horizontally or
vertically, as in an ordinary crossword puzzle, and each
French word will fit in only one place! The English meanings
are arranged according to the number of letters in the French
words, and one French word has been filled in to start you
off. In this puzzle, for instance, you can begin by hunting for
a 4-letter word beginning with T, or a 6-letter word beginning
with O, or a 4-letter word beginning with S. Take it from
there?

8-letter words
  Always   To look for
  Smiles   To bring

6-letter words
  House   To fall
  Objects   To enter

5-letter words
  White   Too
  Red   To have

4-letter words
  Well   Which --?
  Black   Toward
  Large   All
  Alone   Mother

3-letter words
  Your
  That

36

FRENCH LADDERS

To climb these French ladders, you start with the French
word given at either end of the ladder, and by changing only
one letter at a time, go up or down the steps, one by one,
making a new word on each step, until you come out with the
word at the other end of the ladder.

Remember, change only one letter on each step, and leave
all the others in position. Look over the first ladder, which
has been solved for you, and notice how it has been done.
Then try it yourself on the other three.

Maybe it doesn't take
you five steps to get
a BATH TAKEN, but
here's one way to do it!

Not all girls have to
try this many TIMES
to get themselves a
HUSBAND, but then--

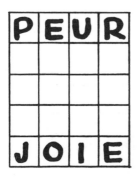

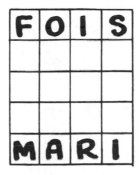

It's not always so easy
to do, but you can
change FEAR to JOY in
a hurry, here!

It's a little bit tougher,
but you can turn this
MOUNTAIN a bright
GREEN!

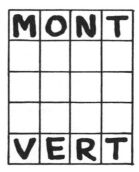

SENTENCE MAZE

Wandering around in this labyrinth is one -- and only one --
complete French sentence. The trick is to hang on to it!
You are to start with the letter D at the top of the maze and
move from letter to letter until you reach the last letter of
the last word, which is the large A in the center square.
You may move up or down , right or left, but you may not
move diagonally and you must not skip over any letter. You
will hit a number of false lures which will try to lead you
into blind alleys. So when you hit a dead end, just go
back and try to pick up the trail again!

START

La phrase est: _____

_____

_____

_____

QUICK CHANGE

Here is a "quick change" word game based on ten pairs of French words with one thing in common. In every case, the second word can be formed by subtracting one letter from the first, leaving all the other letters in position. English clues are provided to help you find the French word. Look at the first pair, which has been worked out for you, and then see if you can do it yourself. . .

BY REMOVING ONE LETTER

1. Turn a large woods
   into a fortification. . . . . **FORÊT → FORT**

2. Change a month of the year
   into a possessive adjective. . . . .

3. Change a possessive adjective
   into an indefinite pronoun. . . . . .

4. Make death only a word. . . . .

5. Make little of fear. . . . .

6. Change "know how"
   into "possess". . . . .

7. Make a court of the heart. . . .

8. Make a month of less. . . . .

9. Change "to show"
   into "to climb". . . . .

10. Turn a school teacher
    into a city official. . . . .

How would you like to run down a few French words? And we
do mean "run down"! In this puzzle, you are going to try to
guess a number of French words, and fit them vertically
into a puzzle block in such a way that one letter from each of
the words will help to spell out a title for the group as a
whole. A sample puzzle has been worked out for you, built
around things that might be found in the living room. When
the French words for "chair," "rug," "lamp," "sofa," and
"piano" are fitted in properly, the word SALON is spelled
out as shown. Take a quick look to be sure you understand
how it is done:

Now see if you can
remember all the
French names for
the days of the week
and fit them into this
pattern!

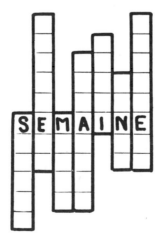

INTERLOCKING CIRCLES

If you can guess the twelve 4-letter French words which fit
the English clues or definitions, you can fill them into the
puzzle pattern in such a way that each word will interlock
with the letters in the words above, below and beside it.
Each word is to be filled into the four squares surrounding
its own number in the puzzle block. But you will have to
watch out for one important detail! Before you have finished,
you'll find that while some words run clockwise around
their numbers, others must be filled in in counterclockwise
direction to give you the right letters for other interlocking
words. The first two have been filled in for you. See if you
can work out the rest!

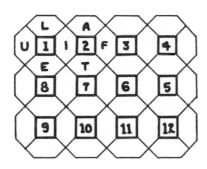

English Clues:

1. A place	7. A lucky number?
2. Does or makes	8. Skin, hide
3. Time (and times!)	9. Loud and high
4. One eye	10. Home of the brain
5. The heavens	11. Of which, of whom
6. Sense, meaning	12. The organ of speech

Remember, if you get stuck,
maybe you've got a right
word going the wrong way!

SQUARE CHAIN

Here's a puzzle that will give you a runaround! Nine French
words are to be arranged in the diagram below, in such a
way that each will run completely around one block of squares,
and provide the first letter (in the numbered square) for the
next word. This word will in turn run across the bridge and
around the next block of squares. English definitions for the
French words are listed below the diagram, and the first
word and the first letter of each of the following words have
been filled in for a starter.

Remember, across the bridge and <u>clockwise</u> around the
square!

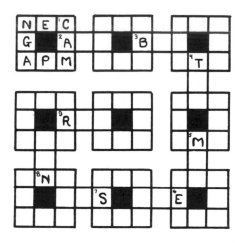

1. Country

2. A four-wheeled vehicle

3. A two-wheeled vehicle

4. In a shy fashion

5. To speak of

6. Expression

7. Simply

8. Food

9. Quickly

WORDS IN WORDS

Here is a word-guessing game in which the trick is to guess
two French words, one of which is inside the other! Each
English clue should suggest two French words, the shorter
of which is spelled out by letters within the longer one. The
letters do not need to be rearranged, and the puzzle squares
will help by showing you the number of letters in the longer
word and the length and location of the "inside" word.

1. A story with you in it!........ `H I S T O I R E`

2. An exciting experience with
    a strong breeze involved......

3. A group of relatives with
    a very large number in it.....

4. Moisturized hot air with
    very little in it..............

5. A celestial being
    surrounded by peril..........

6. A beverage not to be found
    in this religious edifice....

7. A picture with water in it.....

8. A building with a month of
    the year at the front.........

9. Another beverage, this
    time in a number.............

10. There's no accent on the age
    that shows in this face.......

FRENCH TRELLIS

Starting with the words running vertically from the key word RETOURNER, fit French words having the following meanings into the puzzle pattern below. The words run horizontally and vertically in the usual crossword puzzle fashion, and each word will fit correctly in only one place.

3-letter words
End
Street
Word
Our
Upon

4-letter words
Night
Voice
Late
At the house of
With

5-letter words
Cause
Enough
City
To raise
Red
To make
Morning

6-letter words
Still
To leave
To return
Books
Useful (pl.)
(They) know

7-letter words
To listen
To find
General
To return

8-letter words
To look at
To prepare
French

9-letter words
To return (Key word)

10-letter words
To work

11-letter words
To recognize

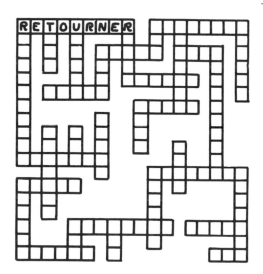

44

WORD MAZE

You have discovered by now that the French have a number of
idioms using the word avoir. In the word maze below,
you can find eight French words frequently used in idioms
with avoir to express physical states or sensations,
emotions, and so on.

Start with any letter any place in the pattern and move
continuously from letter to adjoining letter until you have
completed the word. You may move in any direction,
vertically, horizontally or diagonally -- but you must not
skip over any square to get to another letter, and you may
use each square only once in each word.

Fill in the words you find on the lines below the maze.

Start moving !

E	N	V	I	E
F	A	N	M	P
R	O	I	D	E
F	I	S	U	R
C	H	A	E	B

1. avoir _____   5. avoir _____

2. avoir _____   6. avoir _____

3. avoir _____   7. avoir _____

4. avoir _____   8. avoir _____

45

SCRAMBLED MENU

Here's an easy one! Rearrange the letters in the words below and unscramble M. DuPont's meals for the day!

Le Petit Déjeuner

STEPIT NAPIS   HACCOLTO

_____   _____

Le Déjeuner

SOPINOS

_____

TRÔI DE FOBUE   SOMPEM DE RETER

_____   _____

RUFIT   ROMAFEG

_____   _____

FACÉ AU TALI

_____

Le Dîner

SHOR EVEROUD'

_____

TAGOPE

_____

TIBKEFC   USECA

_____   _____

TEPSIT SOPI

_____

TRATE AU TROCIN

_____

ODD WORDS

An "Odd Words" puzzle challenges you to find the one "misfit" word in a group of words, all but one of which will have something in common. The easiest kind of "odd-word" to find, of course, is one which differs from the rest of the words in its group by some shade of meaning. If, for example, you were looking for the "odd word" in a group containing the French words "blanc, bleu, rouge, joli, noir," it should be easy to see almost at once that the word "joli" is out of place in the group, because all the other words are names of colors.

Here, however, is a number of groups containing "odd words" which are going to be a little harder to find! The words that are out of place in the following groups will have to be weeded out -- not by way of their meanings, but by ferreting out some principle of French grammar or usage to which they do <u>not</u> conform!

How long will it take you to find and draw a circle around the one word in each group which lacks something that all of the others have in common?

1. bon.....petit.....beau.....malade.....grand.....vieux

2. arriver....sortir....montrer....partir...mourir..aller

3. très...trop....tant....beaucoup....assez....combien

4. faire....voir.....être ...rendre....venir....avoir

5. joli....blanc....beau....doux....long....vieux

6. point....quand....jamais....personne....pas....rien

7. appeler...manger...travailler...essayer...lever...
                                          ..commencer

47

QUI VIVE

How about another guessing game with those "adopted" French expressions? Here are 10 once-over-lightly questions about some more of them which you may know. How many can you handle?

1. Mr. Milquetoast is a shy, uncertain sort of character, without much self-confidence. He rarely expresses an opinion and hates having to make decisions. When Mr. M. goes out to dine, would you expect him to order à la carte or table d'hôte? Ans._____

2. Does a billet doux usually come on the first of the month? Ans._____

3. Mrs. Buff-Orphington is serving "potatoes à la mode" at her dinner party tomorrow evening. Does that mean you're going to have to eat your potatoes with ice cream on them? Ans._____

4. "I never want to see you again as long as I live!" said Annabella to her boyfriend, as she shoved him out the door. But when she polished off the evening with a haughty "Au revoir, Mr. Smith!" he was completely confused. Why? Ans._____

5. When you say that Mary Lou has sang-froid, does that mean that she leaves you cold when she sings? Ans._____
   _____

6. When Mrs. Smythe said, "Oh, no! We never have to pay for our theater tickets. My husband works for the manager and he gives us all our tickets au gratin!" -- according to Mrs. S., how was her poor husband getting those tickets? Ans._____
   _____

7. Mr. Hoople was so anxious to hear more of the playing of the great violinist at the concert last night, that he leaped to his feet shouting "Ensemble! Ensemble!" What should Mr. H. have shouted, if he must shout anything? Ans.____
   _____

8. When Belinda looked in the mirror and saw that the wind had played havoc with her hairdo, was she justified in saying, "Oh, dear! My coiffeur is in a terrible state!"? Ans._____

9.   When the plump little lady stood on the pier, waving her hankie after the big liner, and calling out "Bon marché!" what was the dear lady saying? Ans._____

10. When there's a demi-tasse after dinner, does the hostess wear it, do the men smoke it, do the guests drink it, or does the orchestra play it? Ans._____

MAKE YOUR OWN FRENCH TRELLIS!

Have you ever thought that you could make up a crossword puzzle? Perhaps you'd like to start by trying your hand at a French Trellis. They are a good deal easier to construct! Try this one!

1. Begin by starting somewhere in the puzzle pattern where several words intersect, and fit in words that fit. Then work out from there.
2. Watch carefully each time you select a word, to be sure that letters falling into intersecting squares won't be too hard to find in other words.
3. Don't get too attached to a word you've selected. Sometimes it just won't work! Throw it out and try another.
4. Finish with one-word definitions for your puzzle words.

Definitions for your French Trellis:

2-letter words: 4-letter words: 5-letter words: (Cont.)

3-letter words:

5-letter words:

7-letter words:

49

MAKE YOUR OWN SENTENCE MAZE!

The sentence maze is an easy kind of puzzle to make up
yourself. Would you like to try to construct one to try out
on your friends or fellow sufferers in your French group?

Follow these steps and see how you'd do as a puzzle-maker:

1. Begin by thinking up a French sentence eight
   or ten words long, perhaps about how you feel
   about French!
2. Fit it into this maze pattern so that the first letter
   of the first word is in the "start" square, and the
   last letter of the last word comes out in the big
   "finish" square in the center of the pattern.
3. After you have fitted your sentence into the maze
   so that you know it can be solved, go back and fill
   in the rest of the maze with other letters and words
   which may lure the puzzler off on false trails.
4. Remember you can go in any direction, just so
   each letter leads directly to the next. Try not to
   get too complicated!

START

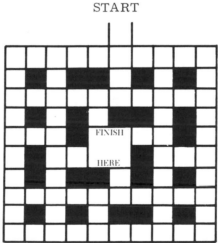

Solution to your Sentence Maze:

_____

_____

MAKE YOUR OWN INTERLOCKING CIRCLES!

If you enjoyed solving interlocking circles puzzles, you
might enjoy making up one of your own. All you have to do is
find twelve four-letter words which can be fitted into this
sort of pattern, and then give clues or definitions which would
identify them.

Perhaps these hints will help you to make one of your own:
1. Begin by making a list of four-letter words. You'll
   have an easier time with a list to refer to!
2. Start with the No. 1 word, and fit them in order.
   Starting in the middle, you'll have to think in all
   directions!
3. Remember that a word may run either way
   around its number. If it won't fit one way, maybe it will go the other!
4. Play fair with your victims. Don't give them words
   that are too tough or unusual, or which they
   haven't yet had!
5. If a twelve-word square is too tough for a starter,
   try a four, six or nine-word square first, by cross-
   ing out the extra squares and re-numbering the
   words in your pattern.

If your puzzle is good enough, maybe the teacher would be
willing to try it out on your classmates.

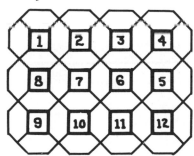

Definitions or clues for your puzzle:

1.	7.
2.	8.
3.	9.
4.	10.
5.	11.
6.	12.

FRENCH-ENGLISH VOCABULARY

The following quick-reference vocabulary contains all the
French words used in the puzzles of *Easy French Vocabulary
Games*. The listing has purposely been made as brief and simple
as possible, and may be used by students to verify intelligent
guesswork or to help themselves over temporary blocks which
might otherwise discourage them from finishing the puzzle.

a: to, at, in
absolument: absolutely
acheter: to buy
adjectif: adjective
âge: age
aîné: elder, oldest
ainsi: thus, so
Allemagne: Germany
aller: to go
allons! let's go!
ami: friend
amour: love
amuser: to amuse
    s'amuser: to enjoy oneself
an: year
ancien, ancienne: old, ancient
ange: angel
Angleterre: England
animal: animal
année: year
août: August
apporter: to bring
apprendre: to learn
après: after
argent: money, silver
arriver: to arrive
artiste: artist
assez: enough
assiette: plate
attendre: to wait
au: to the, at the, in the
aussi: also
automobile: automobile
autour (de): around
autre: other
avec: with
aventure: adventure

avocat: lawyer
avril: April

banane: banana
bas: stocking
beau, bel, belle: beautiful, fine
beaucoup: much, many, a great
    deal
besoin: need
bête: beast, animal
bête: stupid
bicyclette: bicycle
bien: well, very
bien: wealth, estate, property
bientôt: soon
bifteck: beefsteak
blanc, blanche: white
blé: wheat
bleu: blue
bœuf: ox, beef
bois: wood
bon, bonne: good
bonne: maid, servant
bouche: mouth
bout: end, extremity
bras: arm
brun: brown
bureau: desk

café: coffee
cahier: notebook
campagne: country
car: because
carte: card, menu, map
casquette: cap
cathédrale: cathedral
cause: cause

ce, cet, cette: this, that
cela: that
cent: hundred
cerise: cherry
chaise: chair
chapeau: hat
chaque: each
chasse: hunt
chat: cat
château: castle
chaud: hot, warm
cher, chère: dear
chercher: to look for
cheval: horse
chez: at, to, in the home of
chien: dog
chose: thing
ciel: sky, heaven
cinq: five
cinquante: fifty
citron: lemon
classe: class
clef: key
coeur: heart
coiffeur: barber, hairdresser
coin: corner
combien: how much, how many
comme: as, like
commencer: to begin
comprendre: to understand
comte: count, earl
conjugaison: conjugation
connaisance: acquaintance
connaître: to know, to recognize
conte: story, tale
corps: body
côté: side
côtelette: cutlet, chop
cou: neck
couleur: color
coup: stroke, blow
couper: to cut
cour: court, courtyard
cousin: cousin
craie: chalk
crayon: pencil

dans: in
de: of, from
début: debut, first appearance
décembre: December

déjà: already
déjeuner: lunch, breakfast
demain: tomorrow
dent: tooth
depuis: since
dernier, dernière: last
derrière: behind
dessert: dessert
deux: two
devoir: to owe, ought, must
difficile: difficult
dimanche: Sunday
dîner: dinner
dire: to say, to speak
dix: ten
dix-huit: eighteen
dix-sept: seventeen
doigt: finger
donc: therefore, so
donner: to give
dont: of which, of whom
dos: back
doux, douce: sweet, gentle
douze: twelve
duo: duet, twosome

eau: water
école: school
écouter: to listen to
écrire: to write
effort: effort
église: church
élève: student, pupil
elle: she, it, her
employer: to use
en: some, any, of them, of it
en: in, while
encore: still, again
encre: ink
enfant: child
enfin: finally, at last
ensemble: together
entre: between
entrer: to enter
envie: desire
envoyer: to send
errer: to wander, to stray
Espagne: Spain
essayer: to try
est: east

et: and
état: state, condition
Etats-Unis: the United States
été: summer
été: been
être: to be
étudier: to study
eu: had
eux: them, they
exactement: exactly

facile: easy
faim: hunger
faire: to do, to make
fait: fact, deed
fameux, fameuse: famous
famille: family
faut (il): it is necessary
femme: women, wife
fenêtre: window
feu: fire
février: February
figure: face
fille: daughter, girl
fils: son
fin: end
finir: to finish
fleur: flower
fleuve: river
fois: time
forêt: forest
fort: strong, hard
fourchette: fork
franc: franc
français: French
France: France
frère: brother
froid: cold
fromage: cheese
fruit: fruit

garçon: boy, waiter
gare: railway station
gâteau: cake
gauche: left
général: general
gens: people
grammaire: grammar
grand: large, tall, great

grand-père: grandfather
gris: gray
gros, grosse: large, big
guère: hardly, scarcely

habit: clothes, dress, suit
haut: high, tall, loud
heure: hour
heureux: happy
hier: yesterday
histoire: story, history
hiver: winter
homme: man
honte: shame
horreur: horror, shocking thing
hors-d'œuvre: appetizers
huit: eight

ici: here
il: he, it
il y a: there is, there are
île: island
ils: they
imagination: imagination
infinitif: infinitive
intelligent: intelligent
intéressant: interesting
Italie: Italy

j': I (for je)
jamais: never
jambe: leg
janvier: January
Japon: Japan
jaune: yellow
je: I
Jean: John
jeter: to throw
jeudi: Thursday
jeune: young
joie: joy
joli: pretty
joue: cheek
jour: day
journal: newspaper
juillet: July
juin: June

l': the (for le or la)

la: the, her, it
là: there
lait: milk
langue: tongue, language
lapin: rabbit
large: broad, large
le: the, him, it
leçon: lesson
lendemain: the next day
lent: slow
lequel: which
les: the, them
lettre: letter
leur: to them, their
lever: to lift, to raise
lèvre: lip
lieu: place
lion: lion
lire: to read
livre: book
loin: far, distant
loup: wolf
lui: to him, to her, he, him
lundi: Monday
lune: moon
lunettes: glasses

m': me, to me (for me)
ma: my
mai: May
main: hand
maintenant: now
maire: mayor
mais: but
maison: house
maître: master
mal: badly
malheur: misfortune
manger: to eat
mardi: Tuesday
mari: husband
mars: March
matin: morning
mauvais: bad
me: to me, me
médecin: doctor
meilleur: better
même: same
mentionner: to mention

mer: sea
mercredi: Wednesday
mère: mother
mes: my
mettre: to put, to place
midi: noon, south
mien: mine
mieux: better
mille: thousand
moi: I, to me, me
moins: less
mois: month
mon, ma, mes: my
monde: world
    tout le monde: everyone
mont: hill, mount
montagne: mountain
monter: to go up, to climb
montrer: to show
mort: death
mot: word
mourir: to die
mouette: seagull
mouton: sheep, mutton
musée: museum
musique: music

naître: to be born
ne...pas: not
ni...personne: no one
ne...point: not (at all)
nécessaire: necessary
neige: snow
neuf: nine
neuf: new
nez: nose
noir: black
nom: name
non: no
nos: our
notre: our
nourriture: food
nous: we
nouveau, nouvelle: new
novembre: November
nuit: night

objet: object
octobre: October

œil: eye
office: pantry
on: one, people, they
oncle: uncle
ont: have
onze: eleven
or: gold
orange: orange
oreille: ear
ou: or
où: where
oublier: to forget
oui: yes
ours: bear
ouvert: open

pain: bread
paix: peace
panier: basket
papier: paper
paquet: package
parce que: because
parent: parent, relative
parler: to speak
parole: word
parti: departed, left
partir: to set out, to leave
partout: everywhere
pas: (1) not (2) step
pauvre: poor
pays: country
peau: skin, leather
pêche: peach
peine: trouble
peintre: painter
pendant: during
penser: to think
perdre: to lose
père: father
personne: person
petit: little, small
peu: little, few
peur: fear
pièce: piece, room, play
pied: foot
place: place, square
plein: full, open
plume: feather, pen
pluriel: plural

plus: more
point: (1) point (2) not at all
poire: pear
pois: pea
pomme: apple
porte: door, gate
potage: soup, broth
pour: for, in order to, to
pourquoi: why
pouvoir: to be able
premier: first
prendre: to take
préparer: to prepare
présent: present
presque: almost
pris: taken
prix: prize
professeur: teacher, professor
propre: own, clean
proverbe: proverb
puis: then

quand: when
quarante: forty
quart: fourth, quarter
quatorze: fourteen
quatre-vingts: eighty
quatre-vingt-dix: ninety
que: (pronoun) whom, which, that
que: (conjunction) than
quel: what, which
quelque: some, any
question: question
qui: who, which, that
quinze: fifteen

raisin: grape
raison: reason
raisonnable: reasonable
reconnaître: to recognize
recu: received
regarder: to look at
région: region
régulier, -ère: regular
relever: to lift up, to push up
remplir: to fill
rencontrer: to meet
rendre: to return, to make
rentrer: to return, to re-enter

repas: meal
répondre: to respond, to answer
rester: to remain, to stay
retirer: to withdraw
retour: return
retourner: to return, to go back
revenir: to return, to come back
rideau: curtain
riche: rich
rien: nothing
rire: to laugh
risquer: to risk
robe: dress, robe
roi: king
rosbif: roast beef
rose: rose, pink
rouge: red
route: road, way
rue: street
la Russie: Russia

sage: wise, good
salade: salad
salle: room, hall
salon: living-room, parlor
samedi: Saturday
sans: without
savoir: to know
sculpture: sculpture
seize: sixteen
semaine: week
sens: sense, meaning
sept: seven
septembre: September
serviette: napkin
ses: his, her, its
seul: alone
seulement: only
si: if
sien, sienne: his, hers, its
simple: simple
simplement: simply
singulier: singular
six: six
sœur: sister
soi: oneself, himself
soif: thirst
soixante: sixty
soixante-dix: seventy
soleil: sun

son, sa, ses: his, her, its
sont: are
sortir: to leave, to go out
sou: cent
soulier: shoe
soupe: soup
sourire: smile
sous: under, below, beneath
souvent: often
store: window-shade
suave: smooth, suave
subitement: suddenly
substantif: noun
la Suisse: Switzerland
sur: on, upon
sûr: sure
surprendre: to surprise

tabac: tobacco
table: table
tâcher: to try
tant: so much, so many
tante: aunt
tapis: carpet, rug
tard: late, slow
tasse: cup
te: you, to you (fam.)
tel, telle: such
temps: time, weather
tenez: see here! look! I say!
terminaison: ending
terminer: to end, to finish
terre: land, earth
tête: head
the: tea
tien, tienne: thine
tigre: tiger
timidement: timidly
toi: you, to you (fam.)
tomber: to fall
ton, ta, tes: your (fam.)
toujours: always, still
tour: trick, turn
tour: tower
tout: all, whole, every
treize: thirteen
trente: thirty
très: very
trois: three
trop: too much, too many, too

un, une: a, an, one
université: university
utile: useful

vache: cow
vague: wave
vapeur: steam
veau: veal
vendredi: Friday
venir: to come
vent: wind
verre: glass
vers: toward
vert: green
viande: meat
vie: life
vieux, vieil, vieille: old
vif: lively, quick
ville: city, town
vin: wine

vingt: twenty
visage: face, look
vite: quickly, quick
vivre: to live
vocabulaire: vocabulary
voir: to see
voix: voice
votre, vos: your
vouloir: to wish, to want
vouloir bien: to be willing
vous: you
voyager: to travel
vrai: true, real
vraiment: truly, really
vu: seen

y: there
yeux: eyes

zéro: zero

Sentence Maze No. 1, p. 1:

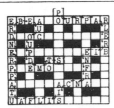

Sentence: "Pour parler bien français, il faut apprendre beaucoup de mots.

Scrambled Grammar, p. 2:

(May be listed in any order)

Substantif	Pluriel
Infinitif	Adjectif
Conjugaison	Présent
Terminaison	Verbe
Singulier	Voyelle

French Anagrams, p. 3:

1.	ami	7.	café
2.	craie	8.	leçons
3.	matin	9.	maison
4.	rien	10.	mois
5.	rue	11.	ciel
6.	amour	12.	mot

Difference of Opinion, p. 4:

1.	store	6.	vague
2.	rue	7.	pain
3.	bout	8.	sage
4.	chose	9.	or
5.	coin	10.	cerise

Odd Words p. 5:
1. rideau(Others:Table setting)
2. une (Others: Furniture)
3. nous (Others: Writing tools)
4. avec(Others: 3rd sing. verbs)
5. livre(Others: Food)
6. jouer (Others: Grammar)
7. ouvert (Others: Classroom)
Rearranged 1st letters:JOURNAL

Acrostic Proverb p. 6:
Key Words:
    1. voici   3. Louvre
    2. sou   4. trop
Proverb:
    "Vouloir, c'est pouvoir."

French Run-Down p. 7:

```
  B      *J
  L       A
  A  *R   U B V R
  N N O B N R E O
  C O U L E U R S
    I G E   N T E
  R E U
     *Interchangeable
```

Ette-iquette, p. 8:

1.	assiette	6.	bicyclette
2.	casquette	7.	serviette
3.	côtelette	8.	mouette
4.	tablette	9.	celle
5.	fourchette	10.	lunettes

    P.S. Alouette

Quick Change, p. 9:

1. pomme...homme
2. père...mère (or vice versa)
3. paix...prix
4. mille...ville
5. panier...papier
6. chapeau...château
7. yeux...feux
8. six...dix
9. vieux...mieux
10. mien...tien
11. tarte...carte
12. main...pain
    P.S. bien...rien

Shades of Meaning, p. 10:
1. sous (under)... sous (money)
2. été (been)... été (summer)
3. aussi (as)... aussi (also)
4. bonne (maid)... bonne (good)
5. monde (people)... monde (world)
6. en (in)... en (some, any)
7. neuf (nine)... neuf (new)
8. point (not)... point (punctuation)
9. bêtes (stupid)... bêtes (beasts)
10. midi (south)... midi (noon)

French Trellis p. 11:

```
Q U I   M A T I N   D
U     O     O     I
A U S S I     U   R
T       L I V R E
R O U T E O   E
E     E   I   A
    R I EN   U N E
C H E R           L
E     E     N     L
L     E       O   E
A N C I E N   S O U S
```

Word Maze p. 12:
Domestic: Wild:
chat vache   tigre loup
chien cheval   lion ours
(in any order)

Artistic French Numbers, p. 13:

Impressionistic rear view:
LE LAPIN!

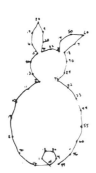

Word-Go-Round p. 14:
(in any order)

ma	ta	cou
mai	tant	coup
mais	tante	coupe
maison	an	ou
ai	tenez	père
son	en	repas
on	nez	pas
oncle	zéro	as
clef	robe	soi
le	beau	soif
effort	beaucoup	faim
fort	eau	
or	au	

Scrambled Nations, p. 15:
1. Allemagne   6. Russie
2. Angleterre   7. Espagne
3. Suisse   8. Japon
4. France   9. Etats-Unis
5. Italie   10. Canada

Interlocking Circles p. 16:

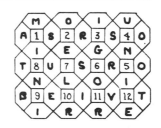

1. mais   5. noir   9. bien
2. rose   6. gros   10. lire
3. gris   7. seul   11. voir
4. nous   8. nuit   12. vite

Acrostic Proverb No. 2., p. 17:
Proverb:
"Paris n'a pas été fait en
un jour."
Key Words:
(1) fort   (4) parti
(2) année   (5) au
(3) juin   (6) passé

Words In Words p. 18:

1. B(LE)U
2. B(LA)NC
3. FR(AN)C
4. SE(MAIN)E
5. P(LAC)E
6. L(UN)DI
7. M(ON)DE
8. TOU(JOUR)S
9. T(ROI)S
10. QU(EST)ION

Square Chain p. 19:

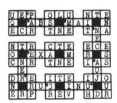

Lost Vowels, p. 20:

1. (E) Les bons élèves étudient leurs leçons pour être bien préparés.
2. (A) La grammaire n'est pas facile, mais il faut la savoir pour parler bien la langue francaise.
3. (I) Il est difficile de lire ainsi si vous n'avez pas d'imagination.
4. (U) Si vous apprenez quelques nouveaux mots tous les jours vous aurez bientôt un vocabulaire plus utile.

Difference of Opinion p. 21:

1. rouge
2. cent
3. tour
4. chat
5. manger
6. car
7. plume
8. parole
9. figure
10. premier

Crypto-French, p. 22:

CBNNV.....pomme
BEZATV....orange
YZAZAV....banane
CBREV.....poire
XRGEBA....citron
EZRFRA....raisin
CVXSV......pêche

French Run-Down p. 23:

A M	N J		J		
V A	O U		J U		
R R	V I		A I	F	S
M O I S D E L A N N É E					
A C L	É M L O V		V P		
I T	C B E Û I		R T		
O	E R T T E		I E		
B	M E		R	E M	
R E	B			R B	
E	R			R	
	E			E	

Word-Go-Round p. 24:

(In any order)

ta	ver	te
table	vers	tel
tableau	verse	telle
blé	se	elle
le	sens	lendemain
eau	en	de
au	ensemble	demain
autre	semble	ma
très	bleu	mai
reste	leur	main
rester	eu	aîné
est	raison	ne
terre	son	net
erre	sont	étable
relever	on	et
relève	ont	
lever		
lève		

Sentence Maze p. 25:

Sentence: Le français est très simple si vous étud-iez un peu.

63

Acrostic Proverb p. 26:

Proverb: "Loin des yeux,
              loin du coeur."

Key Words:
(1) croix   (4) seul
(2) y   (5) donne
(3) lieu   (6) duo

French Trellis p. 27:

```
T A N T           C O U P
E                       E
N O T R E         V I N G T
I                       I
R E S T E R       A R G E N T
      E           R
   P L E I N      R I C H E
      T           I
   J O U R        V O U S
      E           E
   P R O P R E
```

Quick Change p. 28:

1. le-île   6. une-lune
2. cet-cent   7. bas-bras
3. eux-ceux   8. rendre-prendre
4. pas-pays   9. ils-fils
5. main-matin 10. ou-sou

An Ear for French, p. 29:

1. conte:comte   6. vert:verre
2. Jean:gens   7. faim:fin
3. mère:mer   8. cou:coup
4. mon:mont   9. car:quart
5. août:ou   10. sans:cent

Odd Words p. 30:

1. fiancé (Others: Professions)
2. début (Others: Clothing)
3. encore (Others: Arts)
4. suave (Others: Universe)
5. première (Others: Public places)
6. matinée (Others: Earth surface)
7. café (Others: Meats)
Odd words have in common the fact
that all are frequently used in the
English language.

Frenchoglyphics, p. 31:

1. l'élève   6. la porte
2. la craie   7. le livre
3. le tableau 8. la fenêtre
4. le bureau 9. le crayon
5. la chaise 10. le cahier

French Run-Down p. 32:

```
              C
              O O
F    G   U N F S
I T    R   S C I O
L A F A M I L L E
L N R N E N E S U     R
E T E D R     R
   E R P E
      E E
      R
      E
```

Letter Design, p. 33:

REMPLIR
PRESQUE
ARRÊTER
HEUREUX
RETIRER
FENÊTRE
MONTRER
HORREUR
PARENTS
OREILLE
REVENIR

Scrambled Proverbs, p. 34:

1. Tout est bien qui finit bien.
2. Qui ne risque rien n'a rien.
3. Un malheur ne vient jamais seul.
4. Tout nouveau, tout beau.
5. Il faut que tout le monde vive.

Word Maze p. 35:

(In any order)

bouche	joue
cou	langue
dent	lèvre
dos	main
doigt	nez
jambe	pied

French Trellis, p. 36:

```
      T O U J O U R S
      O        B     E
      U        J     U
A U S S I    E  B L A N C
P            T          H
P  B  M A I S O N  Q U E
O  I  E          O  U    R
R  E  R          I  E    C
T O N  E N T R E R  L    H
E         O             E
R O U G E  M      A V O I R
    R      B          E
    O      E          R
    S O U R I R E S
```

French Ladders, p. 37:

FOIS	PEUR	MONT
MOIS	POUR	DONT
MAIS	JOUR	DENT
MARS	JOUE	VENT
MARI	JOIE	VERT

Sentence Maze p. 38:

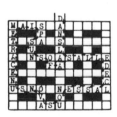

Sentence: Dans la salle de
  classe, nous avons une carte
  mais pas un sofa.

Quick Change p. 39:

1. forêt-fort
2. mai-ma
3. son-on
4. mort-mot
5. peur-peu
6. savoir-avoir
7. coeur-cour
8. moins-mois
9. montrer-monter
10. maître-maîre

French Run-Down p. 40:

```
*V              *M
    E      J      E
    N    D E      R
    D    I U L C
    R    M D U R
S E M A I N E
A D A N   D D
M I R C   I I
E   D H
D   I E
I              *Interchangeable
```

Interlocking Circles p. 41:

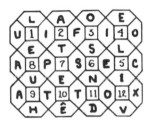

1. lieu   5. ciel   9. haut
2. fait   6. sens   10. tête
3. fois   7. sept   11. dont
4. œil   8. peau   12. voix

Square Chain p. 42:

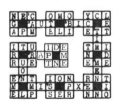

Words in Words p. 43:

1. HIS(TOI)RE
2. A(VENT)URE
3. FA(MILLE)
4. VA(PEU)R
5. D(ANGE)R
6. CA(THE)DRALE
7. TABL(EAU)
8. (MAI)SON
9. (VIN)GT
10. VIS(AGE)

French Trellis p. 44:

```
R E T O U R N E R     R E G A R D E R
E   A   T       O   U   E         E
C   R   I   C A U S E     N U I T   N
O   D   L   H   G       E     R   D
N       E   E   E N C O R E     A   R
N   A S S E Z             A     V   E
A             V I L L E     A
I       F       O             I
T   T   M       A   I         L
R   R   O   I   X     A       L
E C O U T E R         V       E
    U       E         P R E P A R E R
L E V E R         A   C         E
I   E             R             V
V   R             T             E
R     F R A N C A I S   M A T I N
E       I       O   R           I
S A V E N T   S               S U R
```

Word Maze p. 45:

(In any order) avoir... froid, chaud, envie, peur, besoin, raison, faim, soif

Scrambled Menu, p. 46:

Le Petit Déjeuner
petits pains   chocolat

Le Déjeuner
poisson
rôti de boeuf   pommes de terre
fruit   fromage
café au lait

Le Dîner
hors d'oeuvre
potage
bifteck   sauce
petits pois
tarte au citron

Odd Words p. 47:

1. malade (Others: adjectives which regularly precede their nouns)
2. montrer (Others: Verbe conjugated with "être")
3. très (Others: Adverbs of quantity)
4. rendre (Others: Irregular)
5. joli (Others: Irregular adjectives)
6. quand (Others: Negatives)
7. travailler (Others: Verbs of orthographical change)

Qui Vive, p. 48:

1. Table d'hôte probably, since most of his choosing would be done for him on this side of the menu card. Incidentally, it's usually a little less expensive, too.

2. Not unless the amorous author happened to send it then. A billet doux is a love letter!

3. A la mode means "in the fashion". With pie, for example, it seems to be in the fashion to top it with ice cream, but remember that à la mode and ice cream are not necessarily synonymous.

4. The young man has a right to be confused when his lady love bids him goodby forever in one breath, and uses a French phrase for "till we meet again" with the next!

5. Sang-froid means "cold blood" but has to do with coolness under fire or calmness under trying circumstances.

6. According to Mrs. Smythe, her husband is getting his complimentary tickets with cheese or bread crumbs! Would she mean "gratis", perhaps?

7. Mr. Hoople could have saluted the maestro's performance with "bravo!" or some other such expression, but if he wished him to play again, he was probably trying to say "Encore!". French opera-goers are more likely to call out "Bis!"

8. Not unless she knows for a fact that is true. Her coiffeur is the person who dresses her hair. Her hair style is, if she wishes to refer to it that way, her coiffure!

9. The mis-informed little lady is saying "Cheap! Good buy!" The kind of goodbye she wants to say is, of course, Bon Voyage!

10. A demi-tasse being a small cup of black coffee, it is to be hoped the guests drink it!

NTC PUZZLE AND LANGUAGE GAME BOOKS

Multilingual Resources
Puzzles & Games in Language Teaching

Spanish
Classroom Games in Spanish
Easy Spanish Word Games & Puzzles
Easy Spanish Crossword Puzzles
Let's Play Games in Spanish, 1, 2

French
Jouez le jeu
Let's Play Games in French
Classroom Games in French
Easy French Word Games & Puzzles
Easy French Crossword Puzzles
Easy French Grammar Puzzles
Easy French Vocabulary Games

German
Easy German Crossword Puzzles
Let's Play Games in German

Italian
Easy Italian Crossword Puzzles

Chinese
Let's Play Games in Chinese

For further information or a current catalog, write:
National Textbook Company
a division of *NTC Publishing Group*
4255 West Touhy Avenue
Lincolnwood, Illinois 60646-1975 U.S.A.